GRAHAM DANIELS
& JONNY REID

KU-472-746

RACING FOR GLORY

ERIC LIDDELL'S
1924 OLYMPIC STORY

CHRISTIANS IN SPORT

10 Publishing
a division of 10 ofthose.com

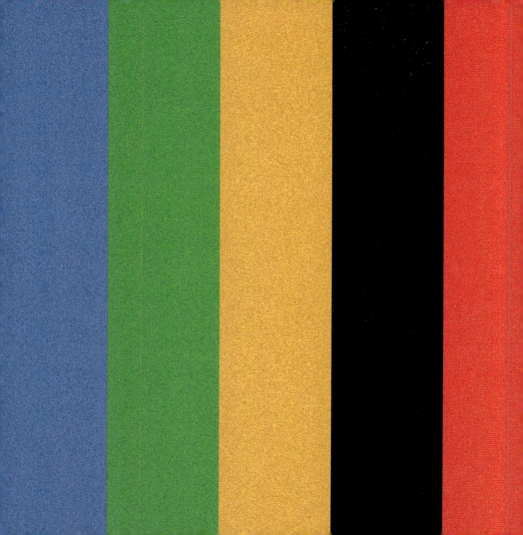

CONTENTS

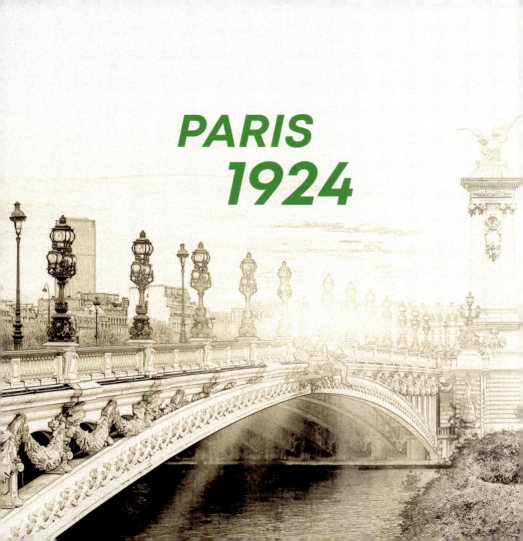

PARIS
1924

"AND NOW, IN ONE HOUR'S TIME, I WILL BE OUT THERE AGAIN. I WILL RAISE MY EYES AND LOOK DOWN THAT CORRIDOR – FOUR FEET WIDE, WITH TEN LONELY SECONDS TO JUSTIFY MY WHOLE EXISTENCE. BUT WILL I?"[1]

Six men lined up for the 100 metres final at the 1924 Paris Olympic Games.

Harold Abrahams of Great Britain was convinced that winning gold would be the defining moment of his life.

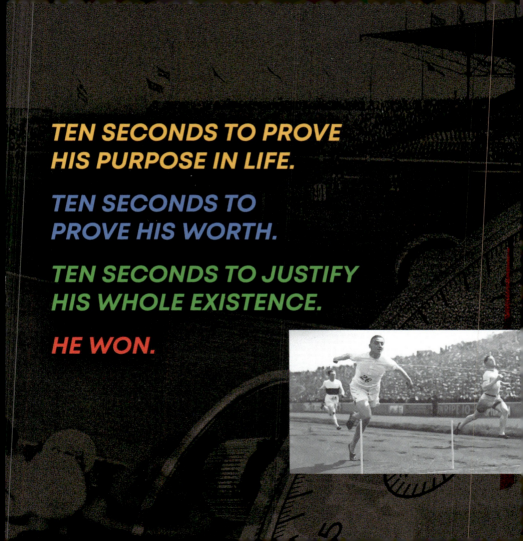

TEN SECONDS TO PROVE HIS PURPOSE IN LIFE.

TEN SECONDS TO PROVE HIS WORTH.

TEN SECONDS TO JUSTIFY HIS WHOLE EXISTENCE.

HE WON.

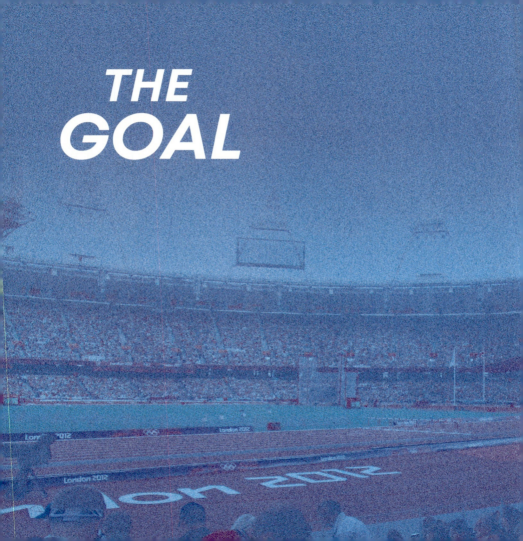

THE
GOAL

The original Olympic motto was "Citius, Altius, Fortius" – Faster, Higher, Stronger. Since 2021, this has become "Faster, Higher, Stronger – Together", acknowledging the unifying ability of sport. Games after Olympic Games, we see countries get behind their representatives as individuals set goals, push boundaries and demonstrate brilliance.

When the wins come, a whole nation celebrates. Who could forget the elation of Super Saturday when Jessica Ennis-Hill, Greg Rutherford and Mo Farah won gold one after another in the 2012 London Olympics? These 44 minutes are recognised as Great Britain's greatest moment at a summer Olympics.[2]

Abrahams' win in 1924 met similar scenes:

> "… the crowd went wild for him [with] 'indescribable enthusiasm' … the cheering lasting 'some minutes, a truly international tribute.' … *The scene of enthusiasm was beyond description, by far the greatest ovation yet seen here …*"[3]

THE
RIVAL

Watching Abrahams in the crowd was his "rival under the same flag", Eric Liddell.

Liddell had chosen to withdraw from this race, his strongest event, where he'd been favoured to win. Applauding, Eric rushed to congratulate his teammate.

Liddell was born in China in 1902, the second son of Scottish missionary parents. Returning to Scotland aged five, he was then educated in England at Eltham College alongside his older brother, Robert. Both brothers captained the school rugby team and it was during these years that others first glimpsed Eric's speed as he set school records every year.

Eric then followed Robert to the University of Edinburgh to study pure science. However, he didn't continue to compete in sport. Liddell said:

> "Six weeks before the first athletic event, a friend, hearing that I had done a little running at school, came round to try and persuade me to enter. I told him I was busy. I had a lot of work to get through and no time for that sort of thing."[4]

This unpromising beginning unfolded in a startling story culminating in the 1924 Paris Olympics just three years later.

On reflection, however, Liddell decided he did want to be involved in sport again, and in his first race at university he ended up winning against seasoned athletes. This continued in nearly every race he competed in, despite his "dreadful" running style. Famously in the 1981 Academy Award-winning film, *Chariots of Fire*, Liddell is seen racing with head pinned back and arms flailing, and this remained even after he enlisted a coach following his first summer of athletics in 1921.

Even before coaching, Liddell had an incredible summer. *The Glasgow Herald* reported his story, calling it "one of the romances of the amateur path. Unknown four months ago, he stands today in the forecourt of British sprinters ... as much because of his extreme grit as because of his pace."[5]

Liddell planned to finish the 1921 season of athletics and return to his studies for the winter. His university friends discovered that he had played rugby at school and decided his raw pace would be useful. By January 1922, he was playing for Scotland. It was said that whilst Eric liked running, he loved rugby. With his warm and generous personality, he thrived on the team nature of the sport.

He played rugby alongside running until the Paris Olympic Games of 1924 came into focus. This is when the fairy tale really began.

THE
CONVICTION

Raised in a Christian home, it wasn't until 1923 that Liddell began to take his Christian faith seriously. He started speaking publicly about his faith, whilst continuing to compete for Scotland in both rugby and athletics. He recognised his sporting talent was a gift from God. In one famous line from *Chariots of Fire*, Liddell says that God "made me fast, and when I run, I feel his pleasure".

Liddell believed God has made and gifted each person, and real joy comes from using those talents for him.

LIDDELL SAYS THAT GOD "MADE ME FAST, AND WHEN I RUN, I FEEL HIS PLEASURE".

Whilst not judgemental of others who took a different view, Liddell took Sabbath observance incredibly seriously and didn't compete on Sundays. But then the blow came.

Liddell was the natural choice to run the 100 metres, 200 metres and the relays for Great Britain in the coming Olympics – he was a sprinter by specialism. But when he saw the 100 metres and the relays included Sunday heats, he immediately made clear he could not compete.

Despite coming under intense pressure to make an exception to his rule, the 22-year-old resolutely put his convictions before personal and even national glory. God mattered more, and Liddell felt compromise would dishonour the one who'd made him fast.

THE
GLORY

Baffling many, Liddell suggested that, along with the 200 metres, he could enter the 400 metres instead. The 400 metres is now known as the "killer sprint" but back then it was seen as folly to sprint the whole way. Eric changed all this. Asked later about his tactics, he explained:

> "The secret to my success over the 400m is that I run the first 200m as hard as I can. Then, for the second 200m, with God's help, I run harder."[6]

Although Liddell wowed the crowds in the heats and the semi-finals, shocking his competitors with his style of sprinting, he was still seen as an underdog in the final. Horatio Fitch, the American champion, set the Olympic record in the semi-final and was the favourite. Commenting on Liddell's tactics, Fitch "couldn't believe a man could set such a pace and finish".[7]

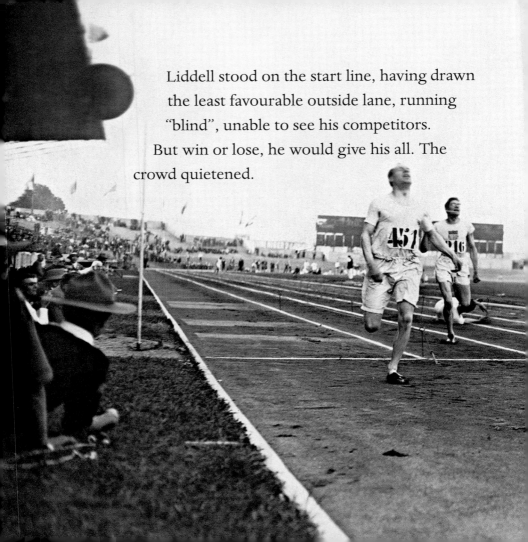

Liddell stood on the start line, having drawn the least favourable outside lane, running "blind", unable to see his competitors. But win or lose, he would give his all. The crowd quietened.

Conserving no energy, Liddell ran the first 200 metres as hard as he could, stunning the spectators. And then, just as he described, he ran the next 200 metres harder.

HE BROKE THE OLYMPIC RECORD SET JUST TWO HOURS EARLIER AND CHANGED THE 400 METRES DISCIPLINE FOR EVER.

Head back and arms out, he passed the tape four metres ahead of Fitch. Coming in at an incredible 47.6 seconds, he broke the Olympic record set just two hours earlier and changed the 400 metres discipline for ever.

THE
MOTIVATION

In 1924, it was considered more noble to be an amateur who tried hard rather than to be trained by a professional coach. Both Liddell and Abrahams were coached, however, and trained hard. In *Chariots of Fire*, Abrahams explains what kept him at it, in all weathers. He ran to prove himself, naming running as his "weapon" against the world. At one point he says:

> "Contentment. I am 24 and I've never known it. I'm forever in pursuit, and I don't even know what it is I'm chasing."

Liddell also ran for glory. He wanted the win too but had a bigger goal – to enjoy God's pleasure in using his God-given gifts. A person can do this even if they lose:

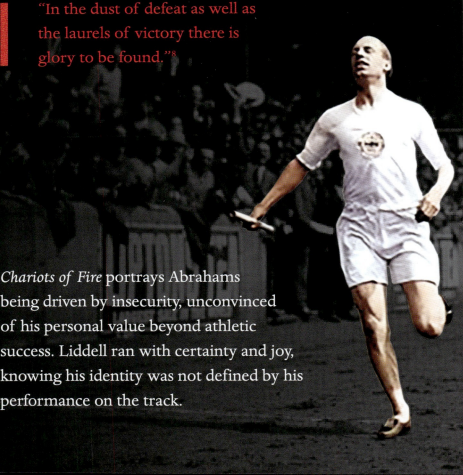

"In the dust of defeat as well as the laurels of victory there is glory to be found."[8]

Chariots of Fire portrays Abrahams being driven by insecurity, unconvinced of his personal value beyond athletic success. Liddell ran with certainty and joy, knowing his identity was not defined by his performance on the track.

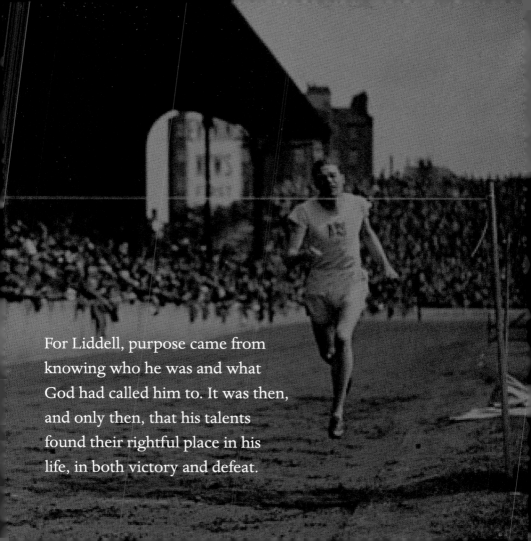

For Liddell, purpose came from knowing who he was and what God had called him to. It was then, and only then, that his talents found their rightful place in his life, in both victory and defeat.

THE
RACE

The Olympic Games began in Ancient Greece. Tradition dates the first Games to 776 BC, although they may well have been older. They continued until AD 393 under the Roman Empire.[9] Athletes have always inspired, and a reference to competitive sport even appears in the Bible – the book Liddell valued so highly.[10]

The Bible author Paul, himself a Roman citizen, wrote:

> "Do you not know that in a race all the runners run, but only one gets the prize? Run in such a way as to get the prize. Everyone who competes in the games goes into strict training. They do it to get a crown that will not last, but we do it to get a crown that will last for ever."[11]

The Apostle Paul likened competition to life. Being familiar with the Bible, Liddell would have known these words well. Liddell was convinced we all have a race to run. He believed each person has a choice to make: to run for momentary glory – crowns that will not last – or to run with eyes focused on the giver of all our gifts, our Creator.

Liddell passionately believed all our striving to be good enough, whether athletically or morally, would ultimately let us down. Success in this life isn't enough to satisfy. We're built for more, and we need our Creator to make us whole.

SUCCESS IN THIS LIFE ISN'T ENOUGH TO SATISFY. WE'RE BUILT FOR MORE.

Liddell returned to China in 1925. He'd always planned to go back to his birthplace and follow in his parents' footsteps sharing the Christian faith.

He found great joy in telling others about his Saviour, Jesus Christ. Jesus died on the cross to take on himself the punishment for sin so we can know forgiveness and eternal life in heaven – that crown which will last for ever. Rather than trying, and failing, to prove ourselves worthy, Liddell explained we simply admit and turn from our wrongdoing and centre our lives on Jesus.

Liddell delighted to share of the God who welcomes anyone

HE FOUND GREAT JOY IN TELLING OTHERS ABOUT HIS SAVIOUR, JESUS CHRIST.

who asks for forgiveness and turns to him in faith; a God who offers new and lasting life.

He wanted all people to know what he'd discovered:

> "Many of us are missing something in life because we are after the second best. I put before you what I have found to be best – one who is worthy of all our devotion – Jesus Christ. He is the Saviour for the young and the old."[12]

When the Second World War broke out, Liddell remained in China and was interned by the Japanese with 1,800 other Westerners. He immediately set about caring for the children in the camp, organising activities and keeping morale high.

In 1945, aged just 43 and still interned, he died of cancer. Although tragically young, Liddell died confident that death was not the end. He was sure of heaven, not because he had proved himself through sporting glory or even through amazing self-sacrifice, but because he had trusted in Jesus who had died to deal with all his wrongdoing and risen again conquering death. His confidence was in his Saviour. Liddell's gravestone included these words which speak of the prize Liddell wanted above all, to be with Jesus in heaven:

> "In his presence is fullness of joy."

Eric Liddell had run his race.

TO FIND OUT MORE ABOUT THE FAITH THAT GAVE LIDDELL HIS SENSE OF PURPOSE, YOU COULD JOIN A COURSE SUCH AS *321 (SPEAKLIFE.ORG.UK/321COURSE)*, WHICH CAN BE DONE IN PERSON AT A LOCAL CHURCH AS WELL AS INDIVIDUALLY ONLINE.

OR YOU CAN READ JESUS'S LIFE STORY FOR YOURSELF TO DISCOVER THE PERSON LIDDELL WAS PREPARED TO GIVE EVERYTHING FOR AT *THE WORD ONE TO ONE (THEWORD121.COM)*.

TO FIND OUT MORE ABOUT THE CONNECTION BETWEEN SPORT AND JESUS, VISIT *CHRISTIANSINSPORT.ORG.UK*.

NOTES

1   All quotes from *Chariots of Fire* (dir. Hugh Hudson, 1981) unless otherwise marked. *Chariots of Fire* tracks the 1924 Olympic bid of Harold Abrahams and Eric Liddell. It won four Academy Awards including Best Original Score. Although the film is based on this true story, the character's words were written for the film.

2   "Olympics: Super Saturday at London 2012 names Greatest British Summer Games Moment", BBC, 25 July 2020. Available at: https://www.bbc.co.uk/sport/olympics/53221821 (accessed 26/01/2024).

3   Rose Staveley-Wadham, "Exploring the Real 'Chariots of Fire' – as Reported in Our Newspapers", *The British Newspaper Archive*, 15 July 2021. Available at https://blog.britishnewspaperarchive.co.uk/2021/07/15/exploring-the-real-chariots-of-fire/ (accessed 02/02/2024).

4   D.P. Thomson quoted in John W. Keddie, *Running the Race: Eric Liddell Olympic Champion and Missionary* (Evangelical Press, 2007), 50–51.

5   Ibid, 62.

6   F.A.M. Webster quoted in John W. Keddie, *Running the Race*, 117.

7   Horatio M. Fitch, "I Was There. The Day We Rode Our Chariots of Fire" in *Modern Maturity*, April–May 1983, 32.

8   This motto of the University of Pennsylvania greatly impressed Liddell. John W. Keddie, *Running the Race*, 103.

9   "History and Origin of the Games" and "Factsheet: The Olympic Games of Antiquity", *Olympics.com*. Available at https://olympics.com/ioc/faq/history-and-origin-of-the-games/what-is-the-origin-of-the-olympic-games (accessed 29/01/2024).

10   This was most probably a reference to the Isthmian Games, held every two years and very similar to the Olympics. Athletes would compete in both major competitions.

11   1 Corinthians 9:24–25, the Bible.

12   Widely attributed to Eric Liddell, see John W. Keddie, *Running the Race*, 157.